-and-woof, protean-shaped article on a hanger and walk to the dressing cubicle. A moment
to cue how this fascinating object marketed as clothing was supposed to relate to a woman's body.
not – and the designer herself an artist. Almost two decades ago, avant-garde clothes designer R i K
New York's SoHo, which was then a name still synonymous with the city's thriving art world. The bright,
the store's design in fact predicted the industrial-luxury look of many galleries to come -- galleries, of
I saw a shopper take an indigo-black, cotton-
cubicle. A moment

eaking, clothes are containers; we are the contents. They protec

PATTERN LANGUAGE { *clothing as communicator*

Judith Hoos Fox, *curator*

artists

Mike Arauz	Patricia Le	J. Morgan Puett and Suzanne Bocanegra	*organized by the*
The Art Guys	Issey Miyake		
Joseph Beuys	Andrew Mowbray	Ramses Rapadas	**Tufts University**
Ecke Bonk	Yoko Ono	Galya Rosenfeld	**Art Gallery**
Cat Chow	Lucy Orta	James Rosenquist	Amy Ingrid Schlegel,
Alba D'Urbano	Maggie Orth / Emily Cooper / Derek Lockwood	Yinka Shonibare	*project director*
Michelle Fornabai		Mimi Smith	
Alicia Framis	John Perreault	Emily Sontag	
Hope Ginsburg	Jody Pinto	Studio 5050	
Patrick Killoran		Rosemarie Trockel	

SIDE FRONT A B
COTE DEVANT
COSTADO DEL FRENTE
SEITL. VORDERTEIL
DAVANTI A LATO
CUT 2

Like painting or traditional sculpture

presentational clothing

communicative if worn in public because

codes, which can refer to age, gender, ra

The clothing we remember often draws its

Clothing can be armor that defends us against hostile invaders.

culture has developed a lexicon for "reading

TABLE OF CONTENT

communicate the personal

and social

The struggle between innocence and

chastity and titillation, exposure and concealment has been going on acr

characteristics that construct **identity.**

othing can be armor that defends us against hostile invaders

ploited as an attribute and conveyor of meaning

CUT HERE FOR A HEM 5/8" (1.5 CM)

Foreword

NEED, DESIRE, SOURCE: THE UNIVERSALITY OF CLOTHING

AMY INGRID SCHLEGEL, DIRECTOR OF THE GALLERIES AND COLLECTIONS, TUFTS UNIVERSITY

In our post-modern, post-industrial, globalized world, clothing may be one of the few truly universal forms of aesthetic expression and practical communication whose symbolic forms can be individually analyzed, decoded, and interpreted as a language or sign system. This is the underlying premise of the exhibition *Pattern Language: Clothing as Communicator*, which offers a sampling of ideas and experiments from the early 1960s to the present from artists born, raised, or based in Egypt, Germany, the United Kingdom, Greece, Honduras, Italy, Japan, the Netherlands, Nigeria, Spain, Taiwan, and the United States—a global assemblage.

As the organizing institution of this exhibition and its national tour, we are delighted to collaborate with guest curator Judith Hoos Fox in this rich selection of artworks that address universal human needs and desires from an astonishing array of source materials.

As each work in the exhibition was selected according to the human needs and desires it fulfils, which the curator has spelled out in the object labels, the exhibition itself had its own set of requirements to reach fruition.

By way of introduction, here is a primer to the exhibition:

Need: shelter, expression, communication, protection, warmth, self-defense, security, class and ethnic differentiation, sexual identification, conformity, concealment, respect, community.

Desire: status, social acceptability, connectedness, camouflage, androgyny, seduction, titillation, modesty, individuality, self-image, self-confidence, non-conformity, fashionability, perfection.

Source: felt, wool, tape measures, zippers, plastic, cotton, Tyvek®, steel wool, Gore-Tex®, acrylic hair, plastic dome, conductive fabric, pigskin, vinyl, silk, waterproof microporous polyester, suede, organza, electric sensors, LEDs, nylon, Twarron® fabric, garment bags, silkscreens, ink, pigment, paper, thread.

Need: Lenders **Desire: Artwork** **Sources:** ○ Bellevue Arts Museum, Bellevue, WA; Michael Monroe, executive director and chief curator ○ Fabric Workshop and Museum, Philadelphia, PA; Marion Boulton Stroud, founder/artistic director, and Janet Samuel, registrar ○ Galerie Monika Sprüth/Philomene Magers, Cologne, Germany; Lilian Haberer, director ○ The Harvard University Art Museums, Cambridge, MA; special thanks to Thomas W. Lentz, director, and Maureen Donovan, chief registrar ○ Jack Tilton/Anna Kustera Gallery, New York, NY ○ The Museum of Fine Arts, Houston, TX; Peter C. Marzio, director, Alison Greene, curator, and Erika Franek, assistant registrar for outgoing loans ○ The Speyer Family Collection, New York, NY ○ The wonderful participating artists and their studios.

Need: Funders **Desire: Supplemental Cash** **Sources:** ○ The Aidekman Family Fund, Tufts University Art Gallery ○ John and Karin Cowl ○ Stuart A. Nielsen ○ Suzanne E. Fox ○ Initial R & D support from Emanuel Lewin of Art Interactive, Cambridge, MA ○ Jacqueline Loewe Fowler ○ Charles O. Wood, III and Miriam M. Wood.

Need: Hard workers, good advice, cost-effective solutions, colleagues
Desire: Vision, assistance, expertise, partners
Sources: Judy Fox, guest curator extraordinaire, who possesses all of the above-mentioned qualities plus a keen knowledge of how to realize her goals, vision, and desires, with a wonderful sense of humor to boot. ○ Doug Bell, our chief preparator, whose expertise in exhibition design has helped realize Judy Fox's vision of the garments as artistic objects and as coded signs; and as registrar, together with meticulous assistance from graduate interns Erin Demerjian and Joanna Groarke, has brought the geographically dispersed grouping of artists and works under one roof at Tufts and coordinated their safe travel to our partnering institutions. ○ Heidi Wirth, our exhibitions, publications, and program coordinator, who dauntlessly and enthusiastically orchestrated a myriad of communications, images, credits, and other catalogue and DVD production design and content issues. ○ Susan Ernst, dean of arts and sciences at Tufts, who supported the idea and ambitions of this project throughout as an apt embodiment of our mission and strategic goals. ○ Martin Oppenheimer, Tufts University counsel, for his expertise in contract law. ○ Paul Sheriff, graphic design consultant, who has designed yet another conceptually resonant and distinctive publication for us. ○ Paul Stern, producer, and Howard Granowitz, editor, of Vox Television for their generous in-kind support to help make the DVD component of the exhibition a reality. ○ Charlie Fox, for his architectural and space design expertise, who was instrumental in realizing a dynamic exhibition design plan. ○ Deirdre Windsor, principal of Windsor Conservation, who generously lent her expertise to ensure that the garments were optimally presented and packed for their journey around the country, and for bringing her graduate intern Yoonjo Lee on board to assist. ○ Kathleen Harleman, director, and Cynthia Voelkl, exhibition coordinator, Krannert Art Museum, University of Illinois, Urbana-Champaign ○ Christopher Scoates, former curator, and Susan Lucke, registrar, University Art Museum, University of California Santa Barbara ○ Lyndel King, director, Gwen Sutter, associate administrator, and Diane A. Mullin, associate curator, Frederick R. Weisman Art Museum ○ Mark Goldsmith, owner/CEO, Goldsmith, Inc., New York City, one of America's oldest and largest producer of mannequins, for in-kind assistance.

CURATOR'S ACKNOWLEDGEMENTS / JUDITH HOOS FOX

My sincere thanks to friends and colleagues who contributed to this exhibition and its program in ways too many to express, including:

Amy Schlegel, who had the courage and confidence to take this project on and make it a reality beyond my dreams.

Winnie Wong and Emanuel Lewin of ArtInteractive, Cambridge – Winnie, who first invited me to think about this idea; Chuck who supported the early development of the show, in all respects.

Jacqueline Loewe Fowler, and other friends, whose confidence in my work and support of it over the years has been most affirming and has made this project happen.

Rachael Arauz, who joined in as associate curator in the R and D phase, sharing terrific ideas, handling masses of material.

Stephanie Davenport, Charlie Fox, Lidney DeBolt Motch, August Ventimiglia, Qi Xu and the rest of the AI gang who worked so hard on the early phase of this project.

Galya Rosenfeld, whom I met via a chance phone call and with whom a natural partnership has grown, involving her work and that of her students, based on shared ideas and passions.

Doug Bell, who stretched in every direction to mastermind the logistics of a complex undertaking.

Heidi Wirth, whose involvement in each step, from the moment the project landed on her desk, has been precise and phenomenal, whose insights have helped shape the result.

Nina Brilliant, Erin Demerjian, Joanna Groarke, Alexandra Irving, and Tuyet Nguyen, interns and graduate assistants who have freely given their time and energy, researching the objects and assisting with loan agreements and with the production of the catalog and exhibition.

Textile Conservator Deirdre Windsor and her graduate intern Yoonjo Lee, whose experience and expertise with garments insured not only peace of mind, but also a wonderful presentation.

Moneta Ho, whose smashing website has taught us all what this medium can do for every aspect of an exhibition.

Andrew Brilliant, my eponymous neighbor – to have such a good friend who is also a terrific photographer!

Paul Stern, whose guidance and generosity through Vox Television have resulted in a terrific DVD for the exhibition, beyond our means and vision.

Howard Granowitz, whose wit, skill, and wisdom we see in the DVD he created, practically from whole cloth.

Robin Givhan, who brought to this catalog a perspective rooted in culture and experience.

Jeff Weinstein, who brought to this catalog an historical context, provocative, and intriguing. Hey Jeff, tell us about that coat, will you?

Lucy Flint, who helped me sound smarter than I am.

Paul Sheriff, whose design for the catalog and exhibition graphics communicates in 2-D the richness and complexity of the ideas expressed in the works in the show.

Kathleen Harleman, Christopher Scoates, and Lyndel King who have insured that the exhibition will have a long life.

The Lenders – the museums and the many artists – who have made works available for the long run of the show.

EVERYMAN

{

Artists across the a

The universality o

Joseph Beuys

Hope Ginsburg

Lucy Orta

ve represented the ordinary human being, from Lascaux's stick figures onwards.

satility of clothing make it an apt form for artists to use in their description of this icon.

Yinka Shonibare

Mimi Smith

Rosemarie Trockel

LUCY ORTA
Nexus Architecture x 8 – Cité La Noue, 1997

YINKA SHONIBARE
Girl/Boy, 1998

JOSEPH BEUYS
Felt Suit, 1970

...ockel resuscitates traditional sources of female pride and empowerment, but she t[akes] [an] unlikely route by inviting a machine to produce her knitted art. How can mechanic[al] [k]nitting elevate the stature of women's domestic work? Machines harness pow[er,] [ex]tend control, command authority, and increase force. By implicitly assigning th[ese] [m]etaphors for virility to the standard feminine job of knitting, Trockel enhances the [st]ature of a woman's task. The involvement of a machine removes knitting from the cate[go] [go]ry of domestic craft and elevates it to a stereotypically male professional activity. A[t] [th]e same time, by assigning a machine the woman's task of knitting, she diminishes the [m]achine's association w[ith] ... [appli]cation, masculine power. Trocke[l] [pl]ays with these incongru[ities] ... [i]n culture, ultimately equal[iz]ing the inequities built into so[ciety] ...

[A] parallel situation explains why ... [uses] computers to design her art. Whil[e] [m]achines relate the physical aspe[cts] ... [th]e stereotypes, computers relate the [m]ental aspects of labor to male stereotypes. Their ... [dire]ctive, precise, and methodical func[ti] [o]ns contrast with women's intuitive, variable, and emotional ways of working. Once again [Tr]ockel subverts habitual attitudes about gender by merging a feminine activity with a mascu[line] [in] the process.

[An]y gender inequalit[ies that] linger are eliminated in a profoundly original manner. [In]stead of attempting to abolish them, Trockel eliminates gender itself. Her sculpture [is] [es]sentially androgynous. There are, for instance, no telltale buttons and zippers on th[e]

ROSEMARIE TROCKEL
Schizo-Pullover, 1988
see credits, page 56

HOPE GINSBURG
Feltmaking, 2000–03

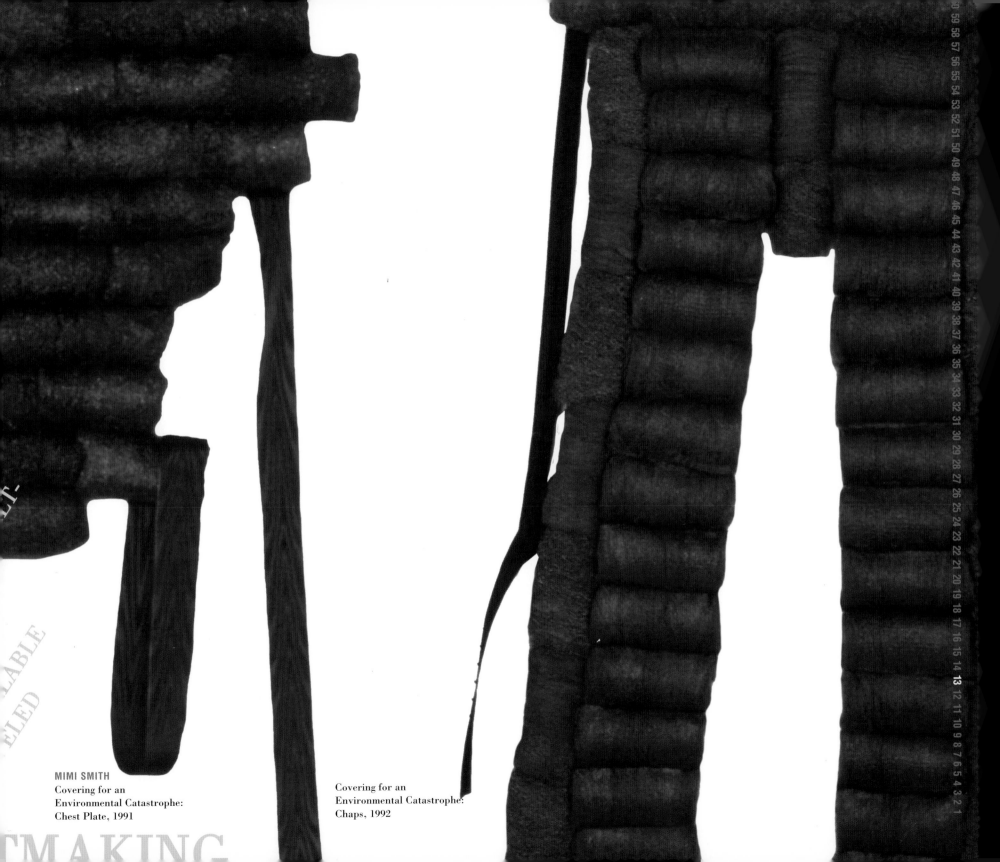

MIMI SMITH
Covering for an
Environmental Catastrophe:
Chest Plate, 1991

Covering for an
Environmental Catastrophe:
Chaps, 1992

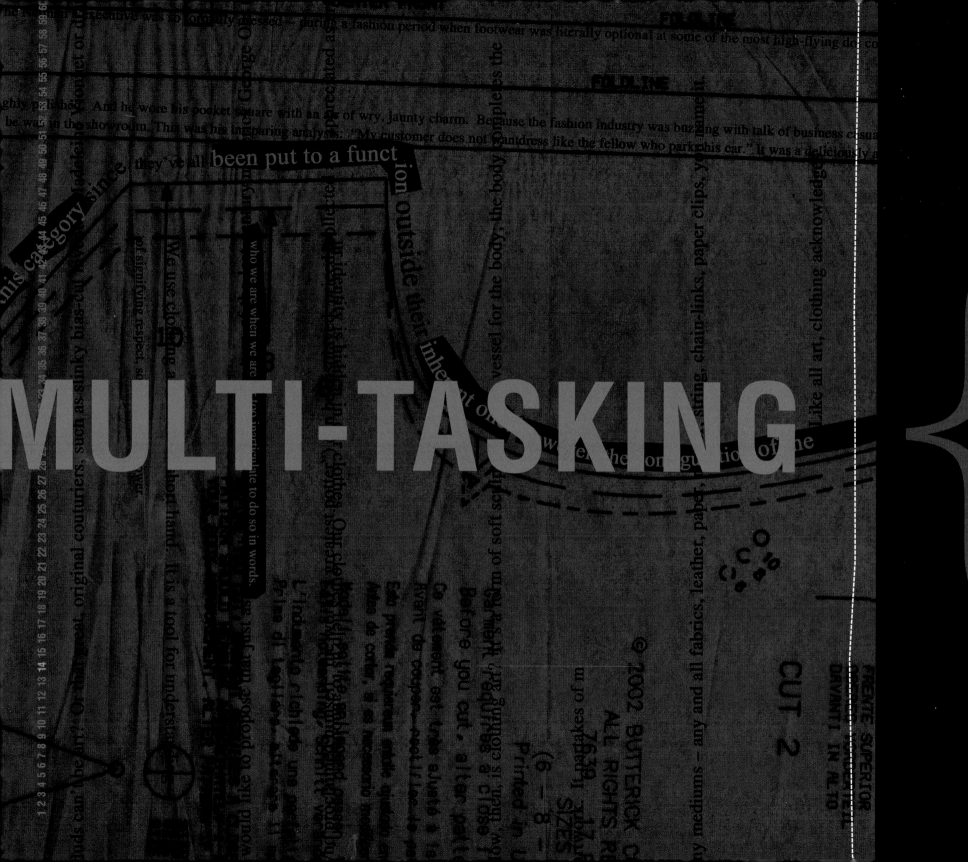

MULTI-TASKING

The Art Guys

Ecke Bonk

ll the works in this exhibition live in this category, in a sense, since they've all been
ut to a function outside their inherent one. However, the configuration of the pieces
ere is fashioned primarily to serve multiple and disassociated activities.

THE ART GUYS
SUITS:
The Clothes Make the Man, 1998
see credits, page 56

T H

CLOT

MAKE

M E

E
ES
HE
N

ECKE BONK
Chess-Jacket (Checkett),
1987-91

"Am I Dressed Appropriately?" ROBIN GIVHAN

One afternoon in New York City, during the mid-1990s, when the fashion industry, a host of swaggering dot coms, and more than a few old guard banks and law firms were championing the advantages of business casual attire, I bumped into a menswear executive from the luxury specialty store Neiman Marcus. We were in the showroom of a designer well-known for his exquisitely tailored clothing. While most of the folks in attendance that day were casually dressed in trousers and a sportjacket, the gentleman from Neiman's was ruthlessly, unapologetically elegant. In fact, he had out-dressed the designer, the only person in the room with an undeniable self-interest in wearing a fine suit.

The Neiman's executive was so formally dressed – during a fashion period when footwear was literally optional at some of the most high-flying dot com companies – that he almost seemed to be a creature from another time. His three-piece suit was cut with Saville Row rigor. His shoes were formal and highly polished. And he wore his pocket square with an air of wry, jaunty charm. Because the fashion industry was buzzing with talk of business casual, the topic was naturally broached while he was in the showroom. This was his unsparing analysis: "My customer does not want to dress like the fellow who parks his car." It was a deliciously accurate, politically incorrect assessment of attire and all its complex meanings.

Just beyond the most fundamental functions of clothing – to provide warmth, protection and, in varying degrees, modesty – lie clues to our place in the culture, hints about our aspirations and our insecurities, information about the social contract. Our identity is hidden in our clothes. As adolescents, as we try to find order in the world, one of the first things we do is search for a tribe. Are we part of the preppy clan with its crewnecks and button-downs? Will we run with the fashionable girls who wear Juicy Couture and Ugg boots? Will we hang with the athletic boys, the rebels, or the geeks? Are we Abercrombie & Fitch or vintage stores? The hippest hip-hop attire can function like armor for the math whiz who fears being called a nerd. A black frock coat and combat boots can express a young man's anger that is too deep for him to understand. A rebel needs something to chafe against. He can't strike out on a unique path if he is dressed in an Izod shirt and a pair of khakis. We are more than the sum total of our wardrobe, but our clothes help us to announce who we are when we are far too inarticulate to do so in words.

Personality and attire are inextricably linked. And as we get older, we use clothing as a kind of shorthand. It is a tool for understanding the world without getting bogged down with details. Clothing becomes a way of signifying respect, sorrow, sexual desire, power. As a culture, we try to deny the importance of clothing. We hate the idea that something so superficial could hold any importance. But instinctively we know that it does. (Our politicians take off their suit jackets and roll up their shirtsleeves when they want to get chummy and informal with voters. They believe that the public discerns earnestness in those wrinkled cuffs and naked forearms.) We tell ourselves that designer labels don't matter and neither do price tags. We only care about what's inside a person's heart. We are only impressed by brain power. Such lies!

Clothes mark certain rites of passage, such as when a young boy moves from short pants to long ones or when a girl buys her first bra. A dress is more than a simple frock when it is a prom dress or a wedding dress. A suit is more than a fashion statement when it is a christening ensemble, a bar mitzvah suit, an interview suit, or a power suit. One of the most moving passages in "A.L.T.," the autobiography of *Vogue* editor-at-large Andre Leon Talley, is a description of how he prepared his father for burial. Talley bought his father a fine silk and mohair Italian suit. He chose a gray silk tie from Charvet. And he selected a pair of white Italian calfskin gloves because his father was a Mason and "Masons must be buried with gloves on." When his father arrived at heaven's gate, he wanted to be sure that he would look his best.

The fashion historian Ann Hollander once noted that the suit was a triumph of civilization. It can be grand and regal, but it also can serve as a kind of political and cultural camouflage – saying nothing suggestive, inflammatory, or suspect. During the Civil Rights protests of the 1960s, black men and women marched in their Sunday bests. Men sat at "whites only" lunch counters wearing a tie and a neatly pressed shirt. The clothes were an extension of their dignity. Even now, there is an element of self-respect that drives a black man, an immigrant, a poor man, to take extra care with his attire, to make sure that he is pulled together, polished, and as natty as possible. Dressing well – or as best as one can – may not ensure that he will be judged fairly, but it denies a critic one more reason to judge him poorly.

Just beyond the most fundamental functions of clothing ... lie clues to our place in the cult

A single garment, pair of shoes or handbag, can speak volumes. Poor Martha Stewart turned up in court to face obstruction of justice charges carrying a Hermès Birkin bag. It was an old favorite. Back when Stewart bought the bag, it was simply an expensive, handmade purse. But time passed and the cultural perception of the bag changed. Over the years, it became a symbol of wealth, luxury, and elitism. Now, the bag has a waiting list so long that there is a wait to get on it. The Birkin – named after the British film actress Jane Birkin – became a storyline on the television series "Sex and the City." Desire for one led one of the characters to lie, curse, and engage in generally bad behavior. The Birkin is no longer just a bag but a $6,000 symbol of exaggerated self-importance. And Martha, essentially accused of assuming that she was above the law, took it to court where she was judged guilty.

Designer labels matter, not because they are true signs of worth, but because they are tools that we use to delineate social and demographic position. Historically, certain colors, patterns, and garments were reserved for the royal court; now certain labels are reserved for – or associated with – the great barons of capitalism and the glamor industry. Gucci has worked hard to convince folks that the label signifies sexy. Hermès prides itself on being perceived as a brand of luxurious understatement. Other brands, such as Chanel or Louis Vuitton, simply allow the wearer to announce: "I've got a lot of money." Sometimes, that's all one needs to say in order to get the best table in the restaurant.

Hip-hop performers instinctively understand the currency of designer labels. Their favorite brands have evolved – from Tommy Hilfiger, Polo, and Nautica, to Gucci, Chanel, and Dolce & Gabbana. Where they once co-opted labels that were symbolic of an upper-middle class sensibility, they now have moved on to labels that are more glamorous and rarified. At first, rappers chose labels that announced their desire to be accepted by the Establishment. Then they chose luxury brands that suggested an intention to be the Establishment. Now, as they launch their own brands – Sean John, JLo – they are redefining precisely what the Establishment is.

Our clothes let others know that we are doing our part to keep the social contract intact. We wear a dark suit to a funeral because that is a way of announcing that we understand the sobriety of the day. Women fret about wearing black or white or red to a wedding because they don't want to insult the bride, upstage her, or simply announce to the other guests that they are socially inept. We perpetuate the important role of clothing in society each time we ask: "Am I dressed appropriately?"

There are some who would insist that clothes are utterly unimportant. To even focus on them is to dance with the devil of superficiality and pretension. To mention a woman's attire is to belittle her, to detract from her intellect, her authority. To notice clothes is to be a snob. But to deny the simple fact that we take note of what the person next to us is wearing is akin to pretending that we don't notice the obvious. Clothing alone does not give us the full picture of a person. It is a thumbnail sketch, an introduction, and a tool for deciding how much more we want to know.

nts about our aspirations and our insecurities, information about the social contract.

ons was in business, I saw a shopper take an indigo-black, cotton-and-wool, protean-shaped article off a hanger

later she called for a saleswoman: "Neither inside nor outside, anything to cue how this fascinating object mark

Kawakubo's clothing art – whether she intends it to be or not – and the designer herself an artist. Al

groundbreaking retail venue for her Comme des Garçons line in New York's SoHo, which was then a name still

minimal, polished-cement space signaled "gallery" instead of shop; the store's design in fact predicted the indust

ourse, being shops that sell art. Comme des Garçons was in business, I saw a shopper take

and-wool, protean-shaped article off a hanger and walk to the dressing cubicle. A moment

later, she called for a saleswoman: "Neither inside nor outside, anything to cue how

CONTAINER/CONTA

practically speaking, clothes are containers; we are the contents. They protect us as They explore way

here is no question that since Marcel Duchamp and the

maturation of modernism, displaying something in a gallery

Our identity is hidden in our clothes. Our

clothes help us to announce who we are

or museum urges us to consider the something, whatever

else we may call it, as art. With one extremely interesting

when we are far too inarticulate to do

exception, the objects in Pattern Language: Clothing

so in words.

Communicator show how art-world artists have work

Michelle Fornabai

Patrick Killoran

{ Practically speaking, clothes are containers; we are the contents. They protect us as we move through our day. Here artists experiment with the nature, configurations, and materials of containers that allow access to the contents in a variety of ways. They explore ways of shutting in the contents and shutting out the world, and vice versa.

Ramses Rapadas

James Rosenquist

Mimi Smith

A GARMENT BAG CLOAKS FASHION BY PROTECTING AND CONCEALING THE CLOTHING IT MAY HOLD. BY BEING TRANSFORMED INTO A GARMENT, THE BAG BECOMES TRANSPARENT CLOTHING. IS IT REALLY TRANSPARENT? CLOTHING HELPS A PERSON FILTER AND PROJECT A SELF-IMAGE. A GARMENT BAG CLOAKS FASHION BY PROTECTING AND CONCEALING THE CLOTHING IT MAY HOLD. BY BEING TRANSFORMED INTO A GARMENT, THE BAG BECOMES TRANSPARENT CLOTHING. IS IT REALLY TRANSPARENT? CLOTHING HELPS A PERSON FILTER AND PROJECT A SELF-IMAGE.

RAMSES RAPADAS
GARMENT(bag)S, 1-3, 2003

JAMES ROSENQUIST
Paper Suit, 1966,
reissued in brown-dyed Tyvek®, 2003

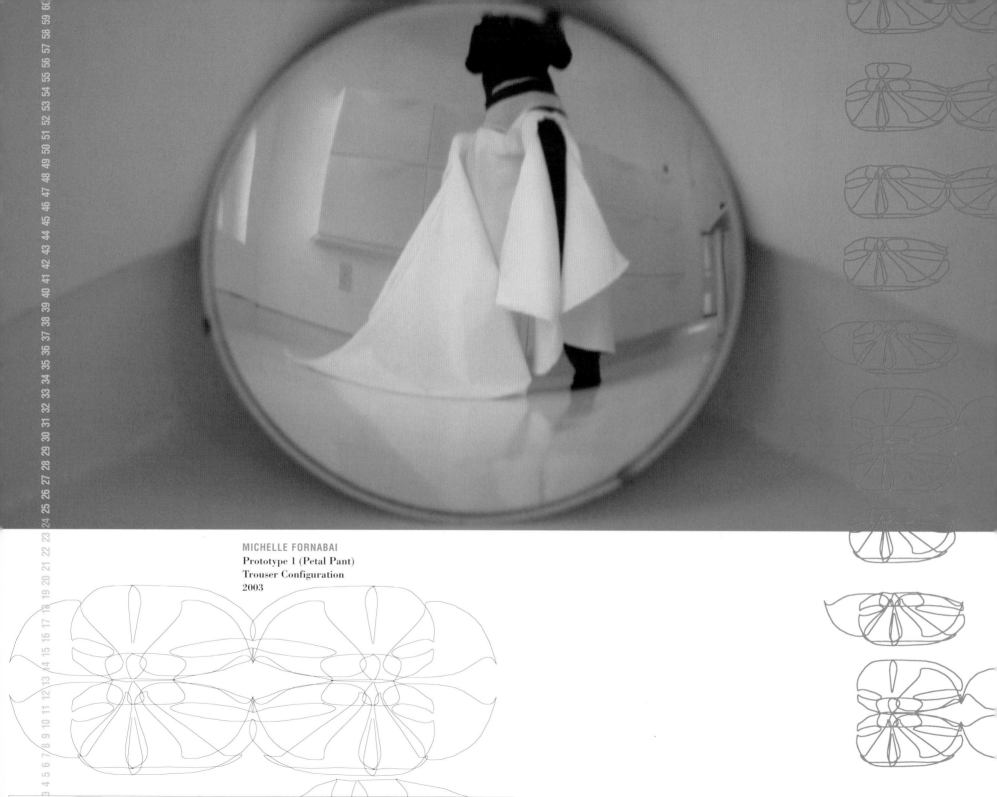

MICHELLE FORNABAI
Prototype 1 (Petal Pant)
Trouser Configuration
2003

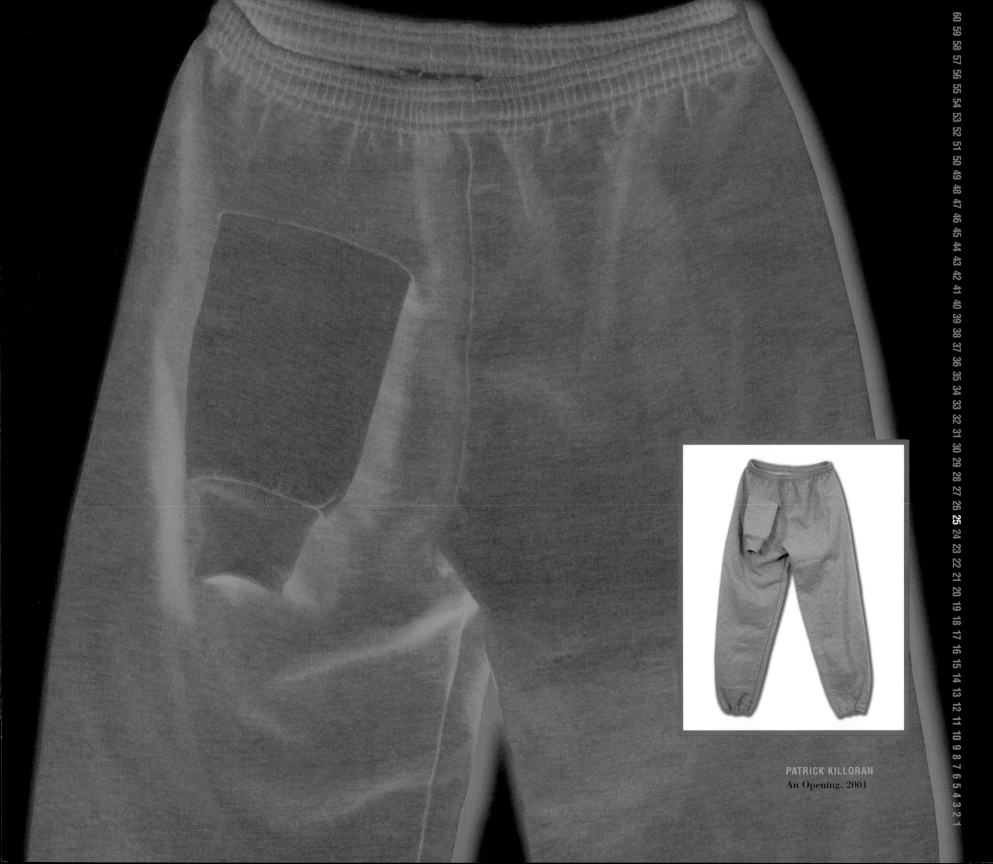

PATRICK KILLORAN
An Opening, 2001

60 59 58 57 56 55 54 53 52 51 50 49 48 47 46 45 44 43 42 41 40 39 38 37 36 35 34 33 32 31 30 29 28 27 26 **25** 24 23 22 21 20 19 18 17 16 15 14 13 12 11 10 9 8 7 6 5 4 3 2 1

SMALL

THE HOLE IN THIS SHIRT ACTS AS A LENS. PULL THE NECK OUT AND POINT THE HOLE TOWARD A SOURCE OF LIGHT. THE IMAGE SHOULD PROJECT ONTO YOUR BODY. WITH PRACTICE, YOU SHOULD FIND WINDOWS, LIGHT BULBS AND CANDLES ALL OVER YOURSELF! THE CLOSER YOU ARE THE LARGER THE IMAGE, AND SO THE MOON WILL ALWAYS BE A BLUE DOT ON YOUR BELLY.

PATRICK KILLORAN
Insight, 1997

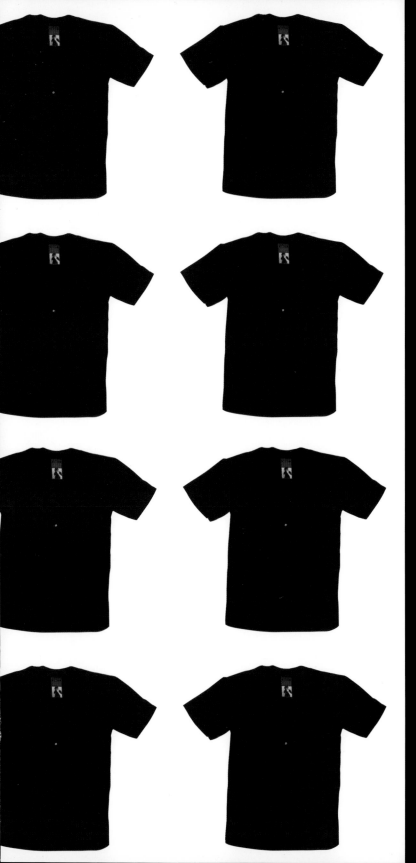

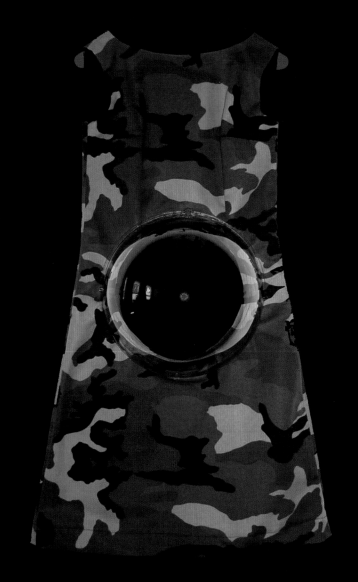

MIMI SMITH
Camouflage Maternity
Dress, 2004

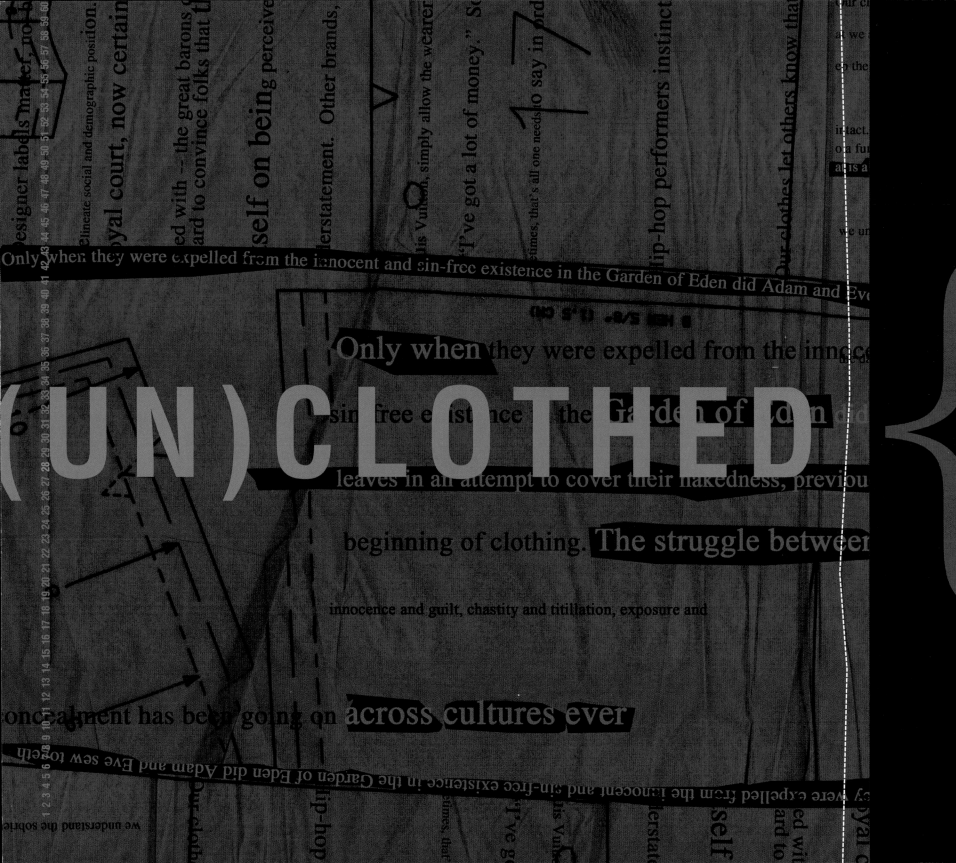

Alba D'Urbano

Yoko Ono

John Perreault

Only when they were expelled from the innocent and sin-free existence in the Garden of Eden did Adam and Eve sew together fig leaves in an attempt to cover their nakedness, previously a state that was just fine. This, in the Bible, is the beginning of clothing. The struggle between innocence and guilt, chastity and titillation, exposure and concealment has been present in cultures ever since.

Jody Pinto

Emily Sontag

YOKO ONO
Cut Piece, 1964

Wear your hair in a totally different way.

Poet John Perreault demonstrates his exciting Hair Line.

Modeled by poet Anne Waldman, the chic primitivism of these

hair inventions for full fashion impact must be worn with

h the bold, bold, totally new bald look. No hair, no make-up. Flesh is the message.

Two units of long brown hair are all you need for a complete wardrobe.

Tied around the head, they become a veil or a hat.

Tied around the arms, a summer blouse that's all sleeves.

Tied around the body just above the breasts, they become a daring mini-dress.

JOHN PERREAULT
Hair Veil, 1969
see credits, page 56

1 2 3 4 5 6 7 8 9 10 11 12 13 14 15 16 17 18 19 20 21 22 23 24 25 26 27 28 29 30 31 32 33 34 35 36 37 38 39 40 41 42 43 44 45 46 47 48 49 50 51 52 53 54 55 56 57 58 59 60

"Hair Shirt" - made of rough hair" and made of hair representing passion, power, energy, worn as a penance

In 1978 Kippy Stroud invited me to make a project at the Fabric Workshop. I made... a shirt come to life in harmony with the body

an attempt to turn the body against itself

hair of the earth - wheat, grass, hay; hair come to life in harmony with the body

representing passion, power, energy, an attempt to turn the body against...

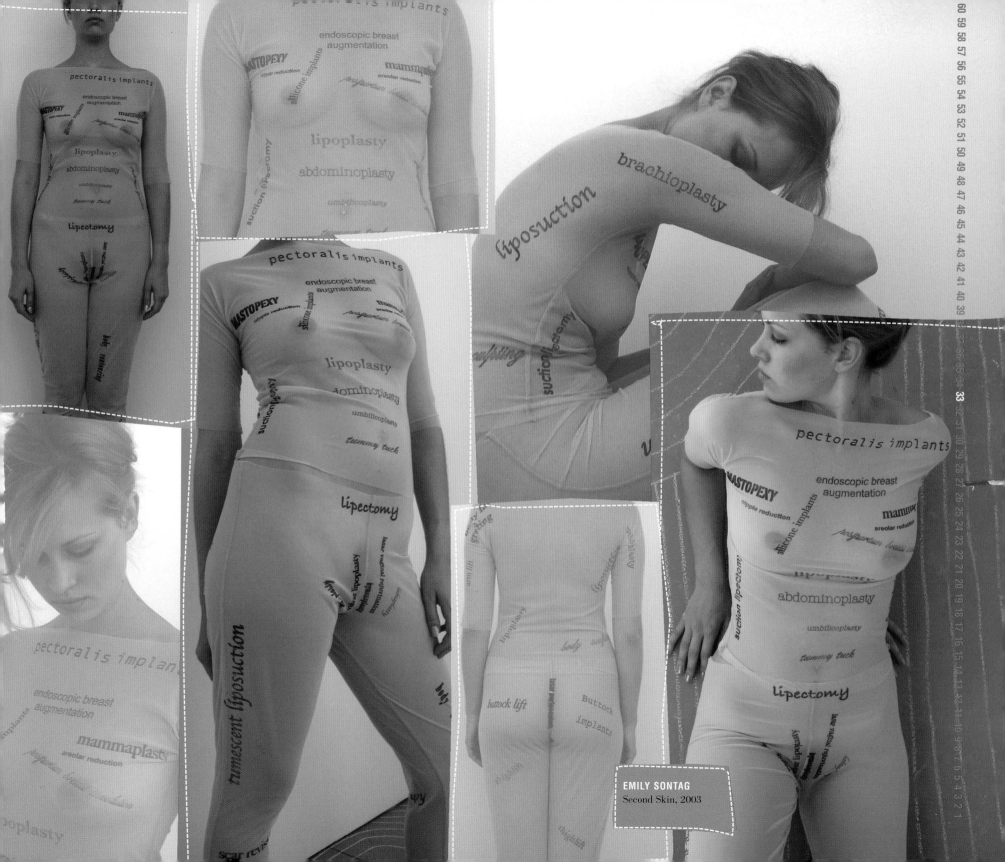

EMILY SONTAG
Second Skin, 2003

Il sarto immortale came into being at a time of individual suffering, a feeling of unease, the desire to escape from my own skin and from being an artist: a situation in which a fundamental incongruity is reflected. On the one hand the capability to get back to the roots of one's own being, to get to know the eve of one's perception and the conditions of the 'I' and to be able to translate them into aesthetic forms is essential, as is the capability of risking psychological fragility; on the other hand the reality of the art market's demands for robustness and managerial abilities. In a certain way it is expected of the artist that he/she shed their skin and sell it with detachment.

ALBA D'URBANO
The Immortal Tailor,
1995-97

Is Clothing Art? JEFF WEINSTEIN

Almost two decades ago, avant-garde clothes designer Rei Kawakubo opened a groundbreaking retail venue for her Comme des Garçons line in New York's SoHo, then a name synonymous with the city's thriving art world. The bright, minimal, polished-cement space signaled "gallery" instead of shop; the store's design in fact predicted the industrial-luxury look of many galleries to come – galleries, of course, being shops that sell art.

Comme des Garçons, Spring, 1989
Maria Valentino/MCV photo

The first year SoHo's Comme des Garçons was in business, I saw a shopper take an indigo-black, cotton-and-wool, protean-shaped article off a hanger and walk to the dressing cubicle. A moment later, she called for a saleswoman: "I need help, I can't see how to put this on." And soon she and her helper emerged, looking for a waist, a belt, a front, a back, an inside or outside, anything to cue how this fascinating object marketed as clothing was supposed to relate to a woman's body. Ultimately they did manage, the brave customer bought the item and early Kawakubo clothing very much like it now can be found in museum collections around the world. Some even call Kawakubo's clothing art – whether she intends it to be or not – and the designer herself an artist.

There is no question that since Marcel Duchamp, displaying something in a gallery or museum urges us to consider that something, whatever else we may call it, art. With one extremely interesting exception, the objects in *Pattern Language: Clothing As Communicator* show how art-world artists have worked with clothing as a concept, a topic, a group of familiar forms manipulated to comment on themselves (Patricia Le's 2004 how-it's-made *Pattern Dress*, Galya Rosenfeld's doubly "smart" all-zipper 1998 *Object Un Dress*); to comment on the way modes of dress define, shield, or promote ourselves (Yoko Ono's filmed performance from 1964 called *Cut Piece*, the Art Guys' peripatetic-billboard 1998 *SUITS: The Clothes Make the Man;* or to embrace both goals (Yinka Shonibare's rich and strange history lesson, 1998's *Girl/Boy*). Yet the exhibition's different creations – many wearable, others not – and recorded performance events lead us to ask a preliminary, crucial question: Why can't any clothing, made by artists or not, be art?

The usual answer is the same that has been invoked to keep so-called craft out of the serious western art club, which is, the more something is meant to be used, the less "art" it can be. So clothing is not art if it's taken off the wall and worn to a dinner party? A quick historical look at the "Is clothing art?" conundrum throws the utility response into deep doubt.

Probably the earliest argument that clothing belongs to the same category as art was made by the late Victorian English designer and theorist William Morris, who tried to convince his contemporaries that the distinction between the fine and applied arts was bogus because the same principles of creation apply – or should apply – to both. His ideal was an aesthetically unified world in which paintings, furniture, wallpaper, and fabric were produced as far from factories as possible, with paints, dyes, materials, and even patterns and themes derived from preindustrial nature and culture. The resulting Arts and Crafts Movement houses, paintings, chairs, books and even suits or dresses, became interconnected artistic equals in what has been called a "style universe."

At the same time, the wider Aesthetic Movement, also in Europe and the U.S., included border-crossing influences from Japan, but its practitioners continued to erase boundaries between fine art and clothing, melding all the arts into a "beauty for beauty's sake" fashion. Ironically, this anti-industry style became personified by a store, Liberty of London, that mass-produced a signature line of increasingly admired printed-silk fabrics, to be sewn by those in the know into loose, flowing, corset-free Aesthetic gowns.

Liberty of London Kimono/V&A
Images, Victoria and Albert Museum

Clothing's tentative invitation to the club of western art was ratified at the beginning of the next century by a number of revolutionary modernist movements. The "art-into-life" impulse of Russian Constructivism was realized by the geometric clothing and textile designs of Lyubov Popova and Varvara Stepanova, two important artists – and women – of that politically fervent time. The Italian Futurists proposed a complete break with behavioral habits of the past, and manner of dress did not escape their scorn. Giacomo Balla's *Futurist Manifesto of Men's Clothing* (1913) passionately decried as passé suits that were "tight-fitting, colorless, funereal, decadent, boring, and unhygienic" and called for the abolition of "wishy-washy, pretty-pretty, gloomy, and neutral colors, along with patterns composed of lines, checks, and spots."

So what should his man of the future wear? "Hap-hap-hap-hap-happy clothes, daring clothes with brilliant colors and dynamic lines." Symmetry in tailoring was banished: "The cut must incorporate dynamic and asymmetrical lines, with the left-hand sleeve and left side of a jacket in circles and the right in squares." Balla wanted this sartorial adrenalin to zip in and out of style as fast as the latest locomotive "in order to encourage industrial activity and to provide constant and novel enjoyment for our bodies."

...There is no question that since Marcel Duchamp, displaying something

But although the artist proudly wore examples of his own design (one photo shows colored triangular shapes sewn into a rather droopy jacket), Balla's pronouncements were never brought into real production. His clothing ideas, the neckties made of wood and embedded with flashing lights (lights still effective in Maggie Orth/Emily Cooper/Derek Lockwood's 1997 *Firefly Dress* and Studio 5050's vests and jackets), were intended more to shock, to jump-start an aesthetic of change. The movement's later art-clothing backed away from the edge: vests by Fortunato Depero from the 1920s are surprisingly traditional shapes decorated with high-contrast but symmetrical appliqué. Only a jacket from the 1930s by Tullio Crali, with no lapels, pockets, or buttons, seems to straddle Futurist innovation and commercial possibility. Still, the Futurists wore their art on their sleeves unequivocally.

The Russian-born, Paris-based modernist who most clearly saw the connection between art and clothing, the "soft Cubist" painter Sonia Delaunay, also divided them, via her commercial fashion success. She was an originator of the concept of prêt-a-porter, or off-the-rack, clothing production and sales. Wearing her zigzag-bordered, early-Deco outfits – made from gem-hued scraps of tulle, flannel, and silk – all around town, Delaunay never doubted that clothing could be art. In 1925, her fashion designs were shown at the Exposition Internationale des Arts Décoratifs, and she gave a pioneering lecture at the Sorbonne about the influence of painting on clothing. The artist also collaborated with the less art-connected designer Coco Chanel; later, Delaunay goods were sold on both sides of the Atlantic, not in galleries, but (surprise!) department stores.

As the 20th century proceeded, it seemed that a piece of hand-made clothing could be art either if it belonged to the prevailing artistic style-universe, or if the hand that made it was attached to an artist. Does that mean factory-made, ready-to-wear duds can't be art? Or that great, original couturiers, such as slinky bias-cut inventor Madeleine Vionnet or dramatic architect of fabric volume Charles James, created objects that cannot be considered art because the creators did not call themselves artists?

I would like to propose that just as a clay bowl or puzzle cup by turn-of-the-last-century maverick George Ohr (who proclaimed himself "the world's greatest potter") can be displayed, priced, collected and appreciated as art, so may articles of clothing, unique or even mass-produced – "multiples," in the vein of artist Joseph Beuys' felt suits. To judge whether they are good or bad art remains the task of viewers, critics, and even those who dare to wear the art in question.

How, then, is clothing art? It's a form of soft sculpture. It's a vessel for the body; the body completes the artwork. It partakes of many mediums – any and all fabrics, leather, paper, rubber, string, chain-links, paper clips, you name it. Like all art, clothing acknowledges history, yet at its most ambitious tries to supercede it.

in a gallery or museum urges us to consider that something, whatever else we may cal

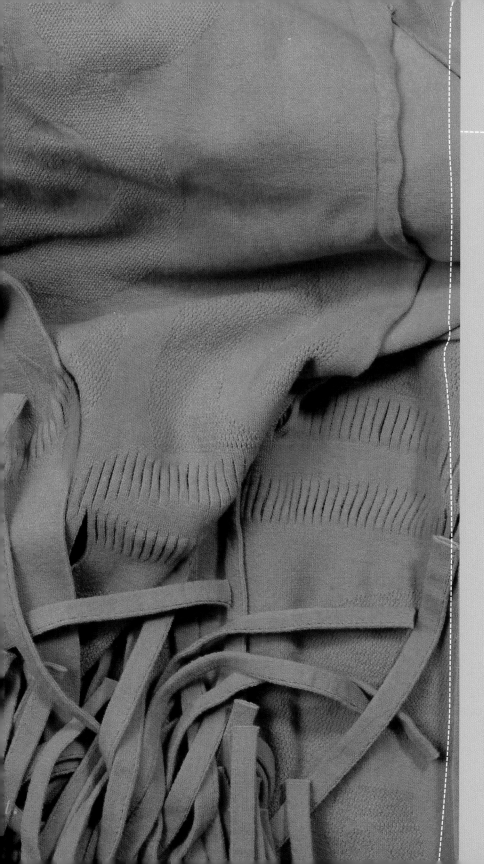

Like painting or traditional sculpture, clothing can be abstract or representational – or neither. (How would you fit a pair of Levis into these categories?) All clothing is "interactive" if worn, communicative if worn in public because it contains codes which can refer to age, gender, race, income, taste, social aptness or "suitability." The clothing we remember often draws its artistic power from reminding us just how striking, how beautiful, created objects can be, and how in clothing's case that beauty multiplies in motion.

In case it isn't clear, clothing is art mostly because it successfully challenges art-or-not categories.

Although museums have collected clothing for years and displayed their homespun smocks and frayed velvet bustles as quaint anthropological artifacts, this began to change about the same time Kawakubo threw her complicated wares up for sale. The Brooklyn Museum showed Charles James' pearlescent taffeta gowns on sculptural pedestals; art critics, not fashion writers, were assigned to review them. Long-time art-worlder Richard Martin took over the galleries of New York's Fashion Institute of Technology and mounted blockbuster shows such as "Fashion and Surrealism," which brought clothing designer Elsa Schiaparelli and artist Man Ray (who was a fashion photographer too) into the same aesthetic arena; Martin went on to replace *Vogue* magazine icon Diana Vreeland and run the popular "fashion shows" at the Metropolitan Museum of Art. Even "serious" art destinations like the Guggenheim Museum attempted to cash in on crossover enthusiasm with a display of Giorgio Armani's wares that many thought turned the Frank Lloyd Wright fixture into a just another Fifth Avenue boutique.

Which brings us to the "one interesting exception" in the *Pattern Language: Clothing As Communicator* exhibition: Issey Miyake. The work shown is called Green Baguette A-POC, ("A-POC" stands for "a piece of cloth") and was part of an art exhibition of pleated fabric tubes – Miyake is a noted master of pleats – from which individuals could fashion their own desired garments. Art? The piece was first shown in a Tokyo gallery and is on loan from the Bellevue Arts Museum near Seattle. Clothing? You may enter a Miyake shop in Tokyo, New York, London, or Paris and buy a shirt or dress that's remarkably similar.

This writer himself had the giddy experience of seeing his much-used black winter coat – I won't bore you with details of who designed it and when – as the very final item, the only male item, in a clothing-as-art museum exhibition a few years back. When the show came down, the coat was returned, nicely cleaned and pressed, and it still sits in the closet, taunting its owner to take it off the hanger, put it on, and walk out into the rain.

Issey Miyake
Green Baguette A-POC, 2003

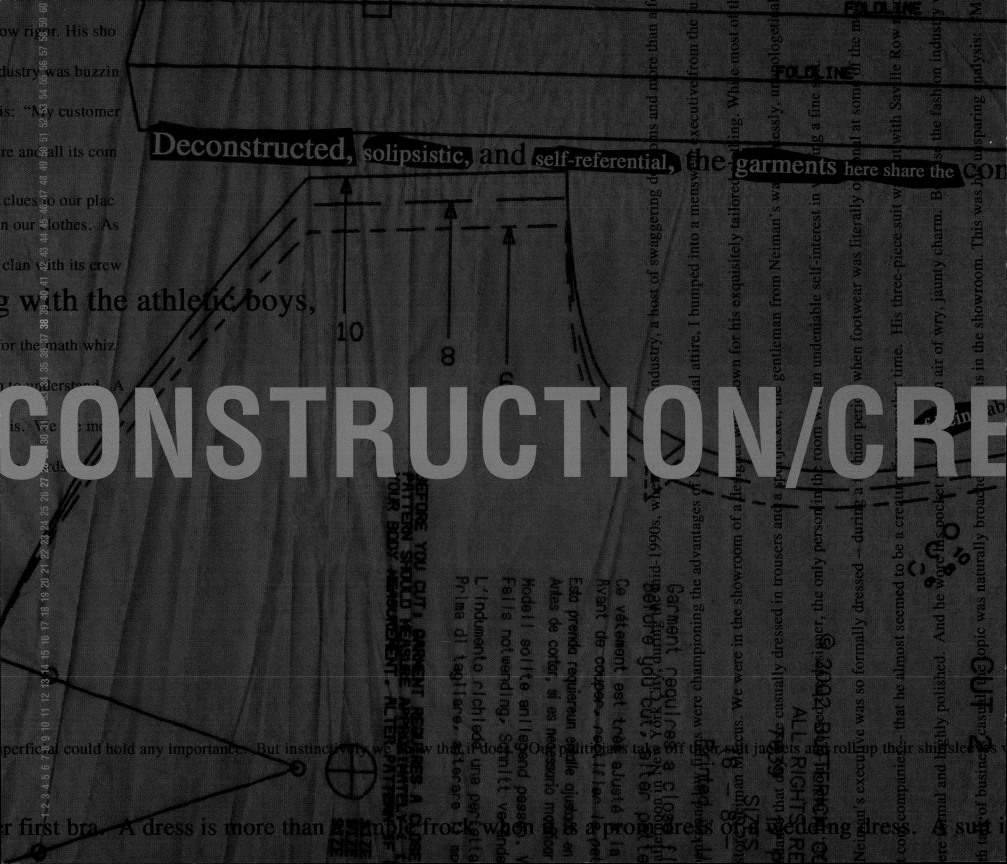

ow rigor. His sho

dustry was buzzin

is: "My customer

re and all its com

clues to our plac

n our clothes. As

clan with its crew

g with the athletic boys,

for the math whiz,

to understand. A

Deconstructed, solipsistic, and self-referential, the garments here share the con

CONSTRUCTION/CRE

perficial could hold any importance. But instinctively we know that it does. Our politicians take off their suit jackets and roll up their shirtsleeves

r first bra. A dress is more than a simple frock when it is a prom dress or a wedding dress. A sui

ion

construction

ATION

{

Patricia Le

Issey Miyake

Galya Rosenfeld

Deconstructed, solipsistic, and self-referential, the garments here share the condition of being about their own construction or creation.

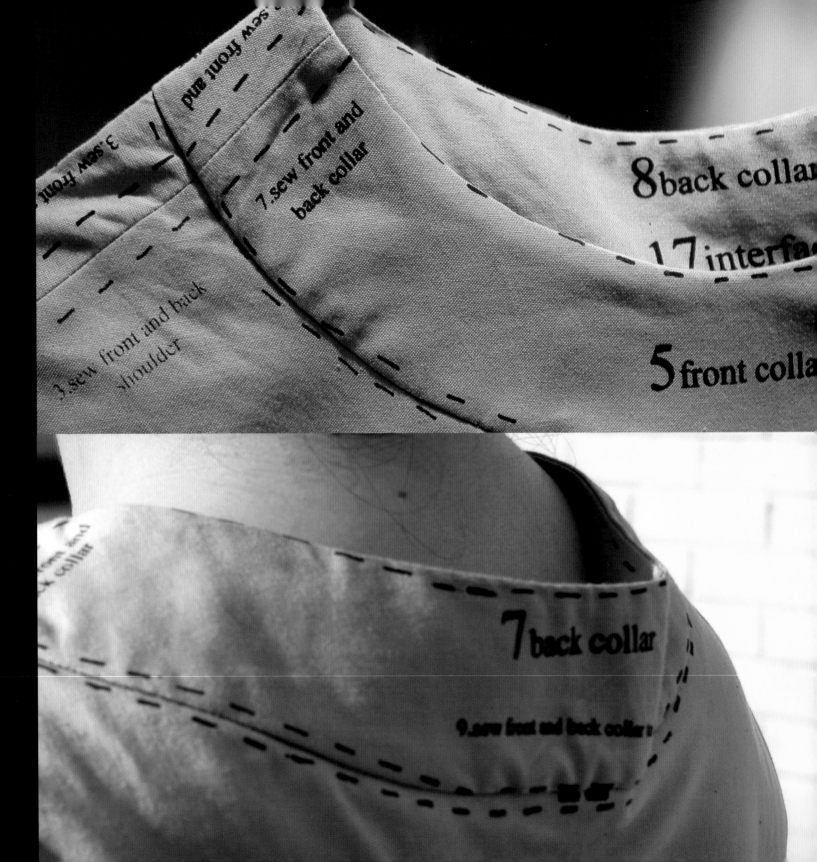

PATRICIA LE
Pattern Dress, 2004

...hink: a thread goes into a machine that, in turn, generates...

...mpleted clothing using the latest computer technology...

...liminating the usual needs for cutting and sewing the fabric...

...he idea stemmed from my desire to make a contribution to...

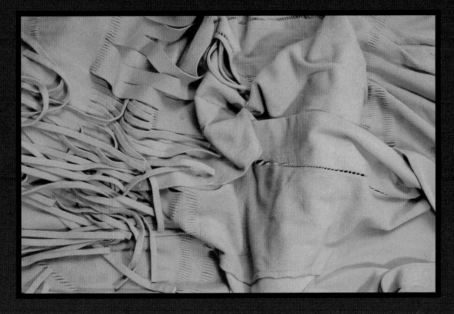

...vironmental protection and the conservation of resources. The process...

...t only cuts down on resources and labour, but is also a mean...

...cle thread... Different dress shapes were knitted in a continu...

...be and the final step in their completion was made by the wearer...

ISSEY MIYAKE
Green Baguette A-POC, 2003
see credits, page 56

GALYA ROSENFELD
Object Un Dress.
1998

This word can also be read as the verb, to dress, implying the action

implyi

Object Un Dress has three states which are reflected in the title. The first state, Object, describes the piece as a thing or "raw material," when the piece

The second state is given by the prefix Un, that implies the action needed to change the piece from its state

appears to be a simp

...ma dress to its state as a pile of zipper (to undo, undress, or unzip)

...e third state, Dress, reflects on the piece as a product, a dress.

needed to convert the pile of zipper into a wearable item... zipper, into a product, the dress, in the space of about three minutes. I was also interested in the formal conversion of a line, the single

continuous zipper, into a sculptural form, the dress. The role of the woman's body within the piece is importan...

...s interested in a piece that can change a so-called raw material, the

IDENTITY

{ *The investigation and assertion ... our culture has developed a lexi... engineering ways that clothing ...*

...against hostile invaders... makes evident the social and ...

investigation

identity is topical theme, well served by the visible and legible expression offered by clothing: our cultu...

...destroying each of the ...

...survive such attacks with her ...

...effective as medieval chain mail. ...swiftly convert into shelters.

...the most fundamental functions of clothing - lie clues to our place in ...

GRAINLINE

STITCHING LINE

STITCHING LINE

SLEEVE FACING
PAREMENTURE DE
VISTA DE LA MAN...
ÄRMELBELAG
MOSTRA PER MANI...
CUT 2

7639
Size
(6 — 8 — 10)

15

...our place in the culture, hints about our aspirations and our inse...

Mike Arauz

Cat Chow

Alicia Framis

Andrew Mowbray

entity is a topical theme, well served by the visible and legible expression offered by clothing:

r "reading" it. Here, artists go beyond choices limited to color or accessories,

used to communicate the personal and social characteristics that construct identity.

Maggie Orth / Emily Cooper / Derek Lockwood

J. Morgan Puett and Suzanne Bocanegra

Studio 5050

MIKE ARAUZ
I AM _____,
2003

ANDREW MOWBRAY
Bachelor's Suit, 2004

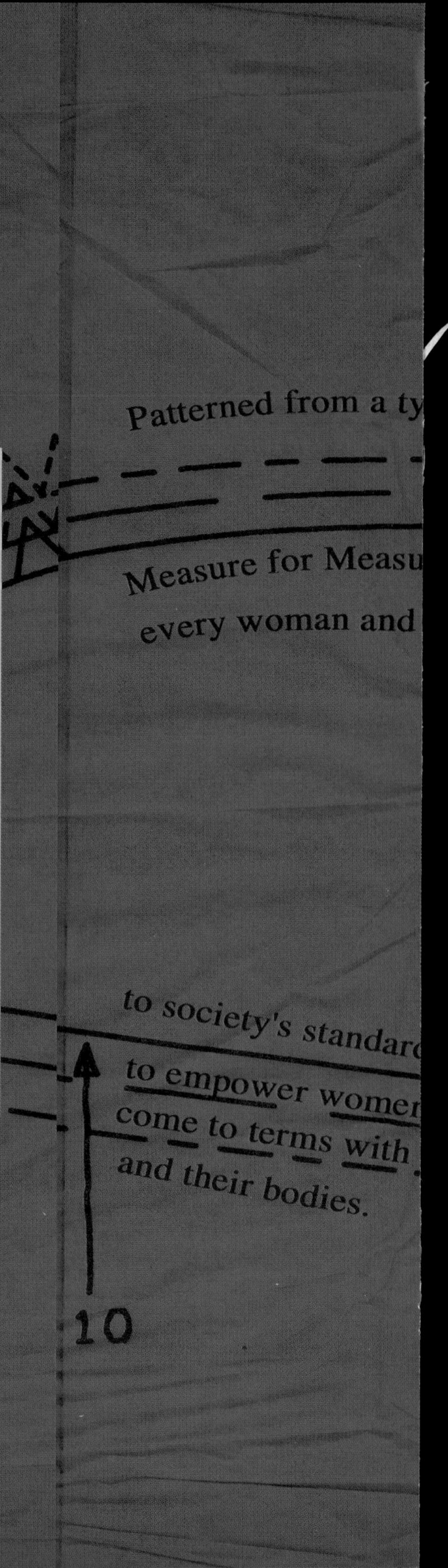

Patterned from a ty[...]

Measure for Measu[...]

every woman and [...]

to society's standard[...]

to empower women[...]

come to terms with [...]

and their bodies.

6   8   10

CAT CHOW
Measure for Measure, 2003

950's house dress,

esents

uggle to measure up

rves to empower

o that they can

hemselves

ALICIA FRAMIS
Anti__Dog Copywriting
Unwanted Sentences, 3 May
2003, Birmingham, 2003

THERE IS NO OTHER FEELING IN THE WORLD

QUITE LIKE BEING SHOCKED BY YOUR DRESS.

INSTEAD, IT PRESENTS A PLACE OF INTIMACY

WITH THE TECHNOLOGICAL AND HEIGHTENED METAPHYSICAL AWARENESS

OF OUR ELECTRICAL NATURE.

IF OUR WORK IN ELECTRONIC TEXTILES PRESENTS

A SORT OF UTOPIA OF TECHNOLOGY,

IT IS NOT SIMPLY AN AESTHETIC ONE.

THIS LITERAL "CLOSENESS" IS ACHIEVED THROUGH

DIRECT MATERIAL CONTACT WITH OUR BODIES.

MAGGIE ORTH / EMILY COOPER / DEREK LOCKWOOD
Firefly Dress, 1997

STUDIO 5050
Hug Jackets, 2004
Love Jackets, 1995/2004

Clothing Communicates JUDITH HOOS FOX

On Tuesday, February 3, 2004, Justin Timberlake apologized in the national media for the "wardrobe malfunction" witnessed by millions of TV viewers of the infamous Super Bowl half-time show two days earlier. The fact that clothing "functions" is something we have known since the expulsion from Eden, and the self-consciousness of the fleeing Adam and Eve continues to be enacted. To be moral means being clothed, yet so many human needs and desires are based on the naked body. Alba D'Urbano manages to have it both ways – her classically styled garments are made of silk and cotton knit printed with full-scale images of female nudes. They reveal nothing and everything. Emily Sontag describes in medicalese some of the countless procedures that are sought and endured to create the ideal physique. While D'Urbano deals with illusion, Sontag refers to our new altered understanding of "reality," a state carefully nipped, tucked, staged, rehearsed, and finally unveiled. John Perreault explores the primal substance of hair: made to protect, used to flirt. Jody Pinto, using actual animal skins adorned with what appears to be body hair, embraces a cultish rite based on mainstream religion – flagellation – in which human ambivalence about the body is played out. Flesh is punished because it is so desired.

Patrick Killoran, in both his sweatpants and his t-shirts, allows covert access to the body. *An Opening* permits easy entry to the most private and protected areas of the male and female. The tiny grommet on the chest of the *Insight* t-shirt makes it function as a camera obscura when it is pulled away from the body. Images from the world are transmitted through the aperture onto the private screen of our torso, conveniently inverted for our easy personal viewing. Mimi Smith's *Maternity Dress* embraces the paradoxical dualities of inside/outside and seen/unseen in clothing. Her camouflage maternity dress exposes the absurdity of the "don't ask/don't" tell policy of the military concerning matters personal and sexual. Whether the pregnant enlisted woman tries to hide her precious burden, or, as in current fashion, lets all see her swelling body, what we really want to see – the baby – and do – touch that amazing body – is still verboten. Maternity clothing, old or new style, is as effective at camouflage as Smith's design.

We announce who we are

through the clothes we wear.

These artists touch on the concept of clothing as container, a concept that James Rosenquist and Ramses Rapadas address directly. Rosenquist's brown paper bag suit, remade in Tyvek® 30 years after its first appearance, suggests that the wearer can be seen as cargo or groceries, the clothes as carrier or container. With Duchampian wit, Rapadas economically conflates garment bag with garment – both of them coverings. He merely eliminates a redundant layer of protective casing. And the container provides more than physical protection. As the public snips off Yoko Ono's garment in her landmark 1964 performance *Cut Piece*, her dignity and composure are also threatened. This universal condition of vulnerability led Joseph Beuys to make a suit with felt – a material symbolic of warmth and survival in his lexicon – to serve as an emblem for the human condition. This garment, drooping on its hanger, has become iconic in the art world. Hope Ginsburg, entranced with the process of making felt, has created custom mittens for her friends and their kids. Through a collection of these synecdoches, she depicts an enclave of unique individuals creating a society. In both cases, with opposite approaches, the artists depict Everyman in felt.

Clothing can be armor that defends us against hostile invaders. Lucy Orta's *Nexus Architecture x 8* makes evident the social and physical connections between people; we are an interdependent species. Yet we also are capable of destroying each other, and Mimi Smith arms us to survive such attacks with her steel-wool chaps and vest, as effective as medieval chain mail. We must adapt to face unexpected threats: Michelle Fornabai brings us elegant garments that swiftly convert into shelters.

The eloquent works of Yinka Shonibare allude to issues of domination, colonization, gender, and role. Andrew Mowbray explores gender and sexuality in his formal white vinyl suit, which recalls Duchamp's *Fountain (1917)* as much as the physician's office with its shiny, slippery white surfaces, urinal-shaped buttons, and delicate, mysterious details. Rosemarie Trockel allows for the multiple identities that constitute each of us – I'm a mother/daughter/wife/curator/laundress/sister/friend/neighbor/etc., for example. We all want to star in our own story, to shine and dazzle, and Maggie Orth and her team of MIT techies put the wearer of their *Firefly Dress* in a perpetual limelight. As the "smart fibers" on the diaphanous layers of fabric brush against each other, they cause the dress to twinkle. Many want to assert themselves as individuals through attire, and both Galya Rosenfeld, in her *Object Un Dress* and Issey Miyake, in his *Green Baguette A-POC*, place certain of the design decisions into the hands of the client – should this garment be a long gown, or a miniskirt? Cat Chow, in *Measure for Measure* – made of neatly and tightly woven measuring tapes – communicates roles, restrictions and responsibilities that have traditionally defined lives, particularly female experiences. Alicia Framis, with her *Anti_Dog Copywriting Unwanted Sentences, 3 May 2003, Birmingham* ensembles, presents the dilemmas of Contemporary Woman to meet expectations that she be vulnerable and sexually alluring as well as strong and independent. Her suite of clothing, inspired by classic fashions of Dior, Chanel, and historic and ethnic costumes, is made of fabrics engineered to keep predators at bay.

It used to be easy to figure out who and what a person was by his or her clothing. Class, education, profession, place of origin, and residence were legible in the turn of a collar, the cut of a suit, the choice of shoes, socks, or tie. But now we are democratized sartorially: jeans and t-shirt are standard issue for all, from CEO to car park kid. In an uninflected and nonhierarchical way, Mike Arauz replaces the subtle signals of style with the blunt clarity of language. He asks participants to put a name to their role within a given community. He gave me a t-shirt that announces in small black uppercase letters that I am a curator, a designation reinforced by my red European glasses and mainly black wardrobe. Tartans were invented to identify family groups, to build pride, and to inflate egos. Interested in redrawing boundaries, J. Morgan Puett and Suzanne Bocanegra used U.S. census data to create two tartans for Manhattan, one based on race, the other on income, the two defining social indicators in our society. In categorizing one's neighbors in this country, race and income are more important than whether one is a MacDougal or a McDuff.

Multi-tasking is a watchword of the times: we talk on the phone while we drive and drink coffee; we listen to music while we exercise and watch TV. Ecke Bonk elegantly prepares us for a game of chess – a Duchampian metaphor for life itself – at a moment's notice. His jacket houses the chess pieces and turns into a handy chessboard when draped over a horizontal surface. The Art Guys ironically subverted the capitalist practice of making consumers pay high prices to sport designer logos by charging corporations to advertise themselves on suits the artists wore to public events throughout the country for a year. We are so busy being busy that we often need help attending to the most basic tasks and emotions. Studio 5050 is helping, by designing clothing programmed to indicate when we have found that special someone.

The works here extend a long trajectory of artists who have exploited clothing as an attribute and conveyor of meaning. An unidentified Roman portraitist took special care to portray the specific outfit of a schoolchild to indicate her gender.[1] William Shakespeare knew: Polonius cautions his son, Laertes, as he departs for college, "Costly thy habit as thy purse can buy./ But not express'd in fancy, rich, not gaudy:/ For the apparel oft proclaims the man;" (*Hamlet*, I, iii.). The donors depicted in 17th century Flemish altarpieces instructed the artists in which fabrics and trimmings to cloak them in their portraits in order to indicate their desired station, though none of these garments actually hung in their wardrobes, nor did the status they indicated necessarily match their own.[2] Today, when Patricia Le integrates the pattern of the dress into the design of the fabric, she economically sums up the concept: clothing communicates.

CHECKLIST OF THE EXHIBITION
Height precedes width, depth varies

MIKE ARAUZ
b.1978, Reading,
Pennsylvania
I AM _____, 2003
Six t-shirts, applied letters
36 x 24 inches
Commissioned by the Tufts
University Art Gallery
Courtesy of the artist

THE ART GUYS
(with Todd Oldham)
Michael Galbreth
b. 1956 Philadelphia,
Pennsylvania
Jack Massing
b. 1959 Buffalo, New York

*SUITS: The Clothes Make
the Man*, 1998
Michael Galbreth's Suit
Wool, silk, cotton, embroidered
logos, plastic buttons
35 x 19 inches (jacket)
47 inches (pants)
Courtesy of the Museum of
Fine Arts, Houston
Gift of Nina and Michael
Zilkha in honor of Lynn Wyatt

Jack Massing's Suit
Wool, silk, cotton, embroidered
logos, plastic buttons
35 x 19 inches (jacket)
47 inches (pants)
Courtesy of the Museum of
Fine Arts, Houston
Museum purchase with funds
provided by the Karen and
Eric Pulaski Philanthropic
Fund of the Houston Jewish
Community Foundation, Mary
and Roy Cullen, and Doris
and Don Fisher

JOSEPH BEUYS
1921, Kleve, Germany -1986,
Düsseldorf, Germany
Felt Suit, 1970
Edition of 100
Felt, sewn
70 x 39 inches
Courtesy of the Busch-
Reisinger Museum, Harvard
University Art Museums,
The Willy and Charlotte Reber
Collection, Patrons of the
Busch-Reisinger Museum Fund

ECKE BONK
b. 1953, Frankfurt, Germany
Chess-Jacket (Checkett), 1987-91
Edition of 32
Gore-Tex® fabric, pigment,
plastic
67 x 38 inches
Courtesy of the Collection of
The Fabric Workshop and
Museum, Philadelphia

CAT CHOW
b. 1973 Morristown, New Jersey
Measure for Measure, 2003
Woven measuring tapes, fishing
line, buttons
72 x 20 inches
Courtesy of the artist

ALBA D'URBANO
b. 1955 Tivoli, Italy
The Immortal Tailor: T-shirt,
1995-97
Digital print, fabric
37 x 27-1/2 inches

The Immortal Tailor: Dress,
1995-97
Digital print, fabric
19 x 37 inches

The Immortal Tailor: Skirt,
1995-97
Digital print, fabric
36 x 37 inches

DVD of collection, transferred
from video, presented on
small monitor
Courtesy of the artist

MICHELLE FORNABAI
b. 1967 Ridgewood, New Jersey
Prototype 1 (Petal Pant)
2003
Laminated high performance
silicone coated nylon fabric,
acrylic rod
28 x 72 inches (pants)
48 x 60 inches (tent)

*Prototype 1 (Petal Pant)
Pattern*, 2003
Ink on silk
Two panels:
l: 93 1/2 x 42 inches
r: 96 1/2 x 42 inches

ISSEY MIYAKE
b. 1938 Hiroshima, Japan
Green Baguette A-POC, 2003
Knit fabric
145 x 19 inches
Courtesy of the
Bellevue Arts Museum

ALICIA FRAMIS
b. 1967 Barcelona, Spain
*Anti__Dog Copywriting
Unwanted Sentences, 3 May
2003, Birmingham Dress*,
2003
Twarron® fabric
197 inches in diameter
Courtesy of the artist

HOPE GINSBURG
b. 1974 Bala Cynwyd,
Pennsylvania
Feltmaking, 2000-2003
Wool
Dimensions variable
Courtesy of the artist

PATRICK KILLORAN
b. 1972 Newtown Square,
Pennsylvania
Insight, 1997
Modified T-shirt, metal grom-
met, paper label
28-1/2 x 35 inches
Courtesy of the artist

An Opening, 2001
Modified sweat pants
42 x 27-1/2 inches
Courtesy of the artist

PATRICIA LE
b. 1981 La Lima Nueva,
Honduras
Pattern Dress, 2004
Cotton blend silkscreened
fabric and dress
41 x 15 inches (dress)
81 x 60 inches (fabric)
Courtesy of the artist

ANDREW MOWBRAY
b. 1971, Boston, MA
Bachelor's Suit, 2004
Vinyl, felt, plastic
68 x 33 inches
Courtesy of the artist

YOKO ONO
b. 1933 Tokyo, Japan
Cut Piece, 1964
Film of performance, trans-
ferred to DVD
Courtesy of the artist

LUCY ORTA
b. 1966 Sutton Coldfield,
United Kingdom
*Nexus Architecture x 8 –
Cité La Noue*, 1997
8 Nexus overalls, waterproof
microporous polyester,
silkscreen print, zippers
79 x 283 inches
Courtesy of the artist

MAGGIE ORTH
b. 1964 Columbus, Ohio
EMILY COOPER
b. 1977 Philadelphia,
Pennsylvania
DEREK LOCKWOOD
b. 1969 Santa Barbara,
California
Firefly Dress, 1997
Embroidered silk, organza,
electronic sensors
54 x 18 inches
Courtesy of Maggie Orth and
International Fashion
Machines, Inc.

JOHN PERREAULT
b. 1937, New York, New York
Hair Veil, 1969
Acrylic hair
Dimensions variable
Courtesy of the artist

JODY PINTO
b. 1942 New York, New York
Hair Shirt, 1978
Edition of 5
Pigment on pigskin
30 x 57 inches
Courtesy of the Collection of
The Fabric Workshop and
Museum, Philadelphia

J. MORGAN PUETT
b. 1957 Hahira, Georgia
SUZANNE BOCANEGRA
b. 1957 Houston, Texas
*The Manhattan Tartan Project,
Phase I and II*, 1999-2001
Wool, statistical data
Variable measurements
of installation
Courtesy of the artists

RAMSES RAPADAS
b. 1971 San Francisco,
California
GARMENT(bag)S, 1-3, 2003
Altered plastic garment bags
and hangers
57 x 80 inches
Courtesy of the artist

GALYA ROSENFELD
b. 1977 Oakland, California
Object Un Dress, 1998
Continuous zipper, stitching
58 x 44 inches
Courtesy of the artist

JAMES ROSENQUIST
b. 1933 Grand Forks,
North Dakota
Paper Suit, 1966,
reissued 2003
Reissued in Tyvek®, shown
with Hugo Boss white long-
sleeved dress shirt and black
necktie
Jacket: 33-1/2 x 35 inches
Pants: 42 x 23 inches
Courtesy of the artist

YINKA SHONIBARE
b. 1962 London,
United Kingdom
Girl/Boy, 1998
Wax-printed cotton textile,
mannequin
71 x 59 inches
Courtesy of The Speyer Family
Collection, New York

MIMI SMITH
b. 1942 Brookline,
Massachusetts
Camouflage Maternity Dress,
2004
Fabric, plastic dome, screws,
metal hanger
47 x 22 inches
Courtesy of the artist and the
Jack Tilton/Anna Kustera
Gallery, New York

*Covering for an Environmental
Catastrophe: Chaps*, 1992
Steel wool, aluminum screening,
fabric, hooks
38 x 26 inches
Courtesy of the artist and the
Jack Tilton/Anna Kustera
Gallery, New York

*Covering for an Environmental
Catastrophe: Chest Plate*, 1991
Steel wool, ribbon, elastic
30 x 24 inches
Courtesy of the artist and the
Jack Tilton/Anna Kustera
Gallery, New York

EMILY SONTAG
b. 1979 San Francisco,
California
Second Skin, 2003
Silkscreen on nylon
pants: 37-1/4 x 21 inches
shirt: 20 x 34-3/4 inches
Courtesy of the artist

STUDIO 5050
DESPINA PAPADOPOULOS
b. 1969 Athens, Greece
ION CONSTAS
b. 1969 Port Said, Egypt
DANA CHANG
b. 1972 Taipei, Taiwan
HELENA PAPADOPOULOS
b. 1965 Athens, Greece
Love Jackets, 1995/2004
Two jackets, infrared receiver
and transmitter module, LEDs,
speaker PIC chip [40kHz signal
and infrared detector]
36 x 32 inches

Hug Jackets, 2004
Two jackets of conductive fab-
ric. LEDs, speaker, PIC chip,
fabric kindly provided by
ULTRASUEDE® from Toray
Ultrasuede (America) Inc.
36 x 32 inches
Courtesy of the artists

ROSEMARIE TROCKEL
b. 1952 Schwerte, Germany
Schizo-Pullover, 1988
Wool
23-1/2 x 26 inches
Courtesy of Gallery Monika
Spruth/ Philomene Magers,
Cologne, Germany

CREDITS

Photo

Mike Arauz, *p.46*: courtesy of the artist

The Art Guys, *p.16*: Alison V. Smith

Joseph Beuys, *p.10*: Michael A. Nedzweski;
© 2004 President and Fellows of Harvard College

Ecke Bonk, *p.17*: In collaboration with the Fabric Workshop
and Museum, Philadelphia

Cat Chow, *p.48*: James Prinz

Alba D'Urbano, *p.34*: Gerhilde Skoberne, Frankfurt/Main

Michelle Fornabai, *p.24*: courtesy of the artist

Alicia Framis, *p.49*: courtesy of the artist

Hope Ginsburg, *p.12*: Ned Matura

Patrick Killoran, *p.25-26*: courtesy of the artist

Patricia Le, *p.40*: Danny Ensele

Issey Miyake, front cover, *pp.36-37, 41*: ©Andrew
Brilliant/www.brilliantpictures.com

Andrew Mowbray, *p.47*: courtesy of the artist

Yoko Ono, *p.30*: courtesy of the artist

Lucy Orta, *p.8*: Passage de Retz, Paris Florian Kleinefen©

Lucy Orta, artist, holds the first Rootstein Hopkins
Chair at London College of Fashion

Maggie Orth / Emily Cooper / Derek Lockwood *p.50*:
© Maggie Orth, 1998

John Perreault, *p.31*: left, © Andrew Brilliant/
www.brilliantpictures.com; right, from "Chic Primitivism
Hair Line" shown at The Fashion Show Poetry Event conceived,
directed, and produced by John Perreault, Eduardo Costa
and Hannah Weiner, Center for Inter-American Relations,
NYC, 1969. Model: Anne Waldman

Jody Pinto, *p.32*: in collaboration with the Fabric Workshop
and Museum, Philadelphia

J. Morgan Puett and Suzanne Bocanegra, *p.52*: courtesy of
the artists

Ramses Rapadas, *p.22*: courtesy of the artist

Galya Rosenfeld, *p.42*: Ilana Rosenfeld

James Rosenquist, *p.23*: courtesy of the artist

Yinka Shonibare, *p.9*: Stephen Friedman Gallery, London

Mimi Smith, *p.13*: Oren Slor

Mimi Smith, *p.27*: courtesy of the artist

Emily Sontag, *p.33*: courtesy of the artist; model:
Laura Eckert

Studio 5050, *p.51*: Ion Constas, Studio 5050

Rosemarie Trockel, *p.11*: courtesy of the artist

Front Cover

MICHELLE FORNABAI
Prototype 1 (Petal Pant), drawing detail

STUDIO 5050
Hug Jackets and *Love Jackets*, drawing detail

ISSEY MIYAKE
Green Baguette A-POC, detail

Back Cover

YINKA SHONIBARE
Girl/Boy, detail

Text

p.11: Linda Weintraub, "Mechanics and Electronics:
Rosemarie Trockel," in *Art on the Edge and Over: Searching
for Art's Meaning in Contemporary Society, 1970s-1990s*,
(Litchfield: Art Insights, Inc., 1997), 143.

p.31: John Perreault, from "Chic Primitivism
Hair Line" shown at The Fashion Poetry Event conceived, directed, and
produced by John Perreault, Eduardo Costa and Hannah
Weiner, Center for Inter-American Relations, New York City,
1969.

p.41: Issey Miyake, from *A-POC Making | Issey Miyake and
Dai Fujiwara* (Germany: Vitra Design Museum, 2001), 68.

p.54, note 1: Diana E.E. Kleiner and Susan B. Matheson,
editors, *Claudia: Women in Ancient Rome*
(New Haven: Yale University Art Gallery, 1996), 198.

p.54, note 2: Yao-Fen You discusses this in an unpublished
paper presented at the College Art Association,
Atlanta, Georgia, 2005.

PROJECT CONTRIBUTORS

Guest Curator and catalogue contributor **Judith Hoos Fox** works independently after nineteen years at Wellesley College's art museum and positions at the ICA Boston, Museum of Art, RISD, the MFA, Boston, and Harvard University Art Museums. Currently she is visiting curator at the Krannert Art Museum at the University of Illinois.

Catalogue contributor **Robin Givhan** is fashion editor for the *Washington Post*.

Amy Ingrid Schlegel, Ph.D., is director of the galleries and collections at Tufts University and project director of the *Pattern Language* tour. Some of her past exhibitions include: *Digital Deluxe*, a survey of east coast digital art practices; *Tseng Kwong Chi: A Retrospective*; *An Unnerving Romanticism: The Art of Sylvia Sleigh and Lawrence Alloway*; and *Post-Pastoral: New Visions of the New England Landscape*. Her current curatorial projects involve Ilya and Emilia Kabakov and Pop women artists. Schlegel's dissertation, "Codex Spero: Feminist Art and Activism in New York Since 1969," focused on Nancy Spero's work and is summarized in the anthology *Singular Women: Writing the Artist* (University of California Press, 2003).

DVD Producer **Paul Stern** is a principal of Vox Television, Inc., a Boston-based production company serving national broadcast, educational, and corporate clients.

Catalogue contributor **Jeff Weinstein** is fine arts editor and popular culture columnist for the *Philadelphia Inquirer*. His writing has appeared in the *New Yorker*, *Artforum*, *Art in America*, *the Village Voice*, and many other publications.

Independent textile conservator **Deirdre Windsor** provides comprehensive conservation services of historic and contemporary textiles. She was formerly the director and chief conservator of the Textile Conservation Center at the American Textile History Museum. In 2001, Windsor was awarded the Rome Prize in Historic Preservation and Conservation from the American Academy in Rome. Recent projects include mounting exhibitions for Historic New England, *Cherished Possessions: A New England Legacy*, and the costumes for *Jacqueline Kennedy: The White House Years*, selections from the John F. Kennedy Library and Museum.

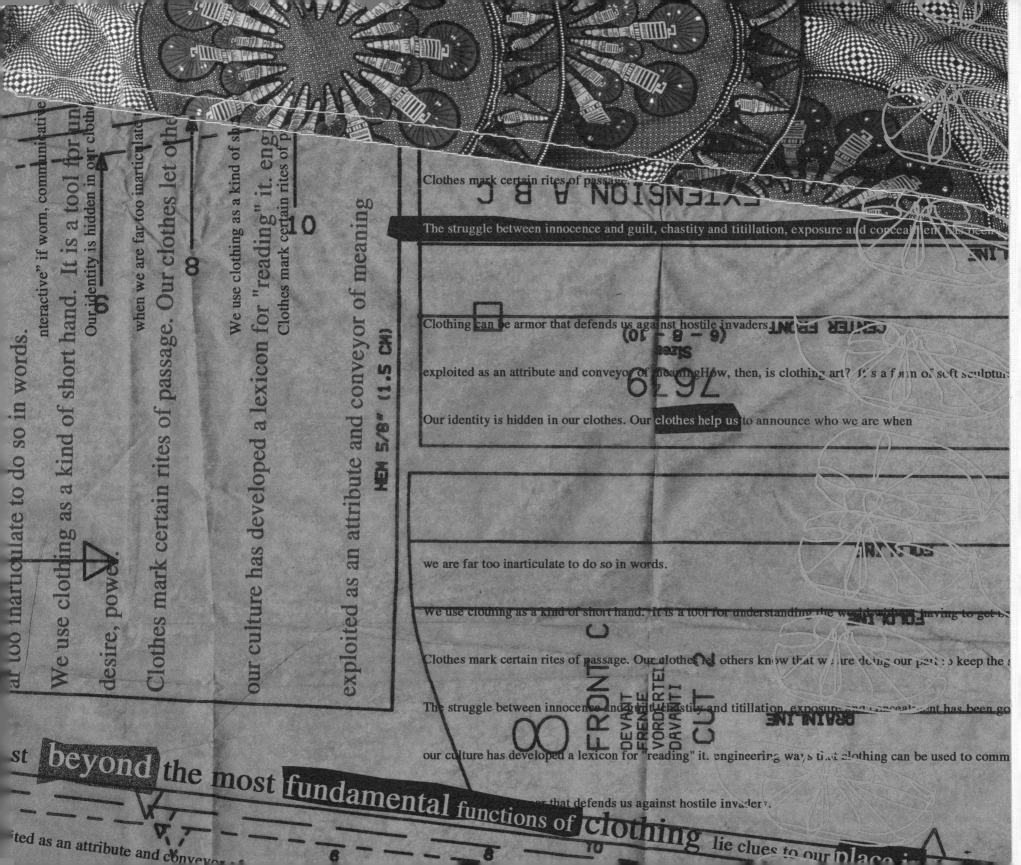